A Dive into DynamoDB Consistent Read Issues

Table of Contents

Chapter 1. Introduction

In this Special Report, we delve deep into the intriguing world of DynamoDB, specifically focusing on consistent read issues. Warmly inviting both technical savants and curious newcomers, we untangle complex concepts, offering a lucid exploration of the underlying mechanics that drive this powerful database service. We discuss real-life case studies, illuminate prevalent issues, and propose well-researched solutions, distilling a technical maelstrom into a comprehensible guide. The complexity of DynamoDB read consistency won't look daunting anymore. Welcome to a report that blends serious technical insight with accessible explanations, essentially a lifeline in navigating the DynamoDB tides. Strap in, there's an engaging exploration ahead.

Chapter 2. DynamoDB: An Overview

Let's set sail on our journey with an exploration of the fundamental characteristics, positioning ourselves to better appreciate our latter discussions about consistent reads.

DynamoDB, part of Amazon Web Services (AWS), offers a fully managed NoSQL database service known for its durability, scalability, and performance. It emerges as a prime choice for businesses that need to handle large amounts of data with low-latency response times.

2.1. Design Goals and Features

Underneath DynamoDB lies a system designed with three explicit goals, namely, performance, scalability, and durability. These goals shape the features that DynamoDB provides:

- Performance at scale: DynamoDB guarantees single-digit millisecond response times at any scale. This feature enables applications to process hundreds of terabytes of data and perform millions of read and write requests per second.

- Automatic scaling: This capability allows the service to manage traffic by dynamically adjusting capacity based on demand, thus minimizing operational overhead and complexity.

- Complete durability and availability: DynamoDB provides built-in fault tolerance, distributing data and traffic across multiple servers to manage hardware failure. It also replicates data across three geographically separate data centers to ensure accessibility and durability.

2.2. How DynamoDB Works

Before diving into DynamoDB's workings, let's grasp some fundamental components.

DynamoDB leverages the principles of the NoSQL data model, focusing on wide-column stores, key-value pairs, graph databases, or document databases. Unlike relational databases, it doesn't employ a typical schema. Tables in DynamoDB are schemaless, except for the primary key—facilitating the storage and retrieval of varied data formats.

The database service operates on two primary key types: Partition Key and Partition and Sort Key (Composite Key).

- The Partition Key, utilized as an input for an internal hash function, determines the partition or physical location where the data is stored.

- The Composite Key comprises both the partition key (hash attribute) and a sort key (range attribute), granting further access flexibility. As DynamoDB hashes and sorts the composite key, it empowers user operations, such as querying or scanning diverse data subsets.

Unlike traditional databases, DynamoDB uses tables, items, and attributes as core components.

- A table is a collection of items, akin to rows in relational databases.

- An item is a collection of attributes, akin to columns in other database models.

- An attribute is a fundamental data element, comparatively a key-value pair in a document database.

2.3. DynamoDB Consistency Models

A key concept to grasp when discussing DynamoDB pertains to its consistency models: Eventually Consistent Reads (default) and Strongly Consistent Reads.

- *Eventually Consistent Reads*: Post a successful write, a subsequent read might reflect the previous state. Nonetheless, consistency across all copies is usually reached within a second—providing high availability and redundancy.

- *Strongly Consistent Reads*: After a successful write, a subsequent read will return the updated data. To avoid inconsistent data reads, use this model.

2.4. Data Access Patterns

Access patterns in DynamoDB can be broadly classified into two types: read and write.

Read operations include `GetItem`, `BatchGetItem`, `Query`, and `Scan`. Write operations encompass `PutItem`, `UpdateItem`, and `DeleteItem`. Each operation's throughput cost varies—a crucial detail when considering the read consistency issues that we're aiming to unravel.

2.5. Conclusion

Understanding the mechanics of DynamoDB prepares us to tackle its concern areas, including consistent read operations. With the DynamoDB stage set, we'll now embark on a deeper dive into read consistency issues, their implications, and the potential solutions. Following chapters will equip you with necessary tools to fully exploit the potential of this powerhouse database service, unraveling the mysteries of read consistency in DynamoDB.

Chapter 3. Consistent Reads in DynamoDB: Breaking the Ice

Let us dive straight in and start grappling with one of the most critical aspects of Amazon DynamoDB - consistent reads.

Amazon DynamoDB is known for its scalability and performance, which it achieves using a distributed and decentralized architecture. However, this comes with a dose of perceptible complexity when it comes to understanding its read consistency model. The aim here is to shed light on the complex process in the simplest possible language. For this, first, we need to understand the distinguishable aspect of 'Read Consistency.'

Chapter 4. Read Consistency: The Fundamental Notion

A simplified definition of 'Read Consistency' suggests, it happens when one receives the most recent data written to a location, irrespective of the node from where the data is read. This may sound simplistic but when operating in a distributed, multi-node environment like DynamoDB, achieving this consistency is not an easy task.

Chapter 5. Eventual Read Consistency and Strong Read Consistency

DynamoDB offers two types of read consistencies: Eventual Read Consistency and Strong Read Consistency. Knowledge about these types will form the cornerstone of our exploration.

Eventual Read Consistency refers to a scenario in which the read operations (following a write operation) may not reflect the latest data immediately. However, the system guarantees that once all the updates are propagated to all nodes, subsequent reads will reflects the most recent data, hence the term 'Eventual.'

On the contrary, Strong Read Consistency promises the return of the most recent data immediately after a write operation occurs. When a Strongly Consistent Read is requested, DynamoDB silos data across all nodes, ensuring they mirror the latest write operation.

Chapter 6. The Mechanics behind Eventual Read Consistency and Strong Read Consistency

Given DynamoDB's distributed architecture, it uses partitioning and replication for data storage. When a write operation is performed, the data is written to all nodes simultaneously. If an Eventual Consistency Read occurs before the write operation is complete on all nodes, the data received may not reflect the most recent changes.

Alternatively, when Strong Read Consistency is requested, DynamoDB ensures that all nodes have received the latest write operation before allowing a read, which ensures the return of the most current data.

Chapter 7. Case Study: Consequences of Eventual Read Consistency

Let's study the implications of Eventual Read Consistency with an example. Imagine an online ticket booking system where Peter successfully books a ticket. Soon after, Emily attempts to book the same ticket. If an Eventual Read Consistency model is in use, Emily's request could be approved as the system may not have updated Peter's booking across all nodes.

Chapter 8. Case Study: Impact of Strong Read Consistency

Now, let's study Strong Read Consistency with the aforementioned example. If Strong Read Consistency is employed, Emily's booking attempt would be denied as Peter's booking information would have been updated across all nodes before Emily could complete her booking.

Chapter 9. Solving Consistency Dilemmas with DynamoDB

As we understand both Read Consistency models in DynamoDB, the choice between the two depends on the specific use case and requirements. If the business application requires immediate reflection of data changes ensuring data accuracy at all times, Strong Read Consistency is the way to go, albeit with a minor impact on read performance due to the additional latency.

For applications where minor inconsistencies can be tolerated, Eventual Read Consistency provides a lower latency and higher throughput.

In conclusion, DynamoDB offers flexibilities to make the right choice based on the business needs. Understanding these read consistency models is decidedly crucial to navigate the DynamoDB landscape. It is hoped that this chapter has introduced and simplified the concept of consistent reads, providing a stepping stone to the intricate depths of DynamoDB.

Chapter 10. Case Study: Unveiling Commonly Encountered Read Consistency Issues

In the world of NoSQL databases, Amazon's DynamoDB has carved a niche due its unparalleled scalability, gigantically high performance, and unremitting reliability. Although it counsels tranquility to developers handling big data, there is an area often causing confusion - consistent reads. Perplexing behaviors, sporadic issues and ensuing risks frequently arise from a lack of understanding the underworking of read consistency in DynamoDB.

10.1. Know Your Reads: Eventual and Strongly Consistent

By default, DynamoDB tosses its weight behind eventual consistency. Quick and lightweight, an eventually consistent read may sometimes fetch data that's slightly out-of-date, as it doesn't always wait for the latest write to propagate across all storage locations in the proliferation of the replication process.

In contrast, a strongly consistent read guarantees up-to-the-minute data, but with slightly increased latency owing to the law of the CAP theorem, which demands a trade-off between consistency and latency. In the vast majority of situations, the eventual consistency model is adequate. However, when consistency is paramount - such as with bank transactions or a bid increment in a live auction - strongly consistent reads become the norm.

10.2. A Real Case: The E-Commerce Website

Suppose you are overseeing the backend of a global e-commerce website. User sessions and cart details are stored in a DynamoDB table, employing eventual consistency for reading data due to its advantage of reduced read capacity unit (RCU) consumption.

One day, support tickets start piling up, coming from customers complaining that the items they just added to their shopping carts aren't showing up. Meanwhile, other customers report that the cart is displaying outdated item quantities. Plunging into the problem, your engineering team suspects the cause is likely tied to the use of eventually consistent reads.

10.3. Decoding The Issue

In scenarios where consistency matters, the trade-off between reduced latency and perceptible inconsistencies can create real problems. For instance, in the user-experienced shopping cart inconsistency mentioned earlier, the time-lag caused by eventual consistency is perceivable by the user and could dent the overall user experience, causing confusion and loss of confidence.

With an eventually consistent read, there's a possibility that your read request hits a node that hasn't received the latest writes yet, which in turn can make certain operations risky, such as decrementing a stock counter or updating item quantities in a cart. In our e-commerce case, the read inconsistency is causing trouble since post-write, the updated cart information is not always reflected immediately.

10.4. Implementing Strong Read Consistency

On identification of this issue, your team decides to switch to a strongly consistent read model for retrieving cart information. Despite knowing it might consume double the RCU and might increase latency, your team is ready for the trade-off to ensure accurate cart data for users. After the changes are made, the complaints about cart-related issues are notably reduced.

10.5. Conclusion and Further Advice

When it boils down to deciding the type of read consistency, the stakes are high indeed. Make the call based on the specific requirements of your business logic. In cases where inconsistency can hinder user experience or operations, like the one mentioned, opt for strong consistency.

In general, the rule of thumb is to use eventual consistency where slight inconsistencies can be tolerated, as it comes with the cost-effectiveness of consuming fewer RCUs. However, understand that it might increase the likelihood of stale or non-existing data being served in a slender time window.

The careful study of these case scenarios fortifies our grasp on the understanding of read consistency in DynamoDB. With this ammunition in our arsenal, the risk of missteps is greatly reduced, and the opportunity to design more robust and user-friendly applications significantly increased.

Chapter 11. The Internals: How DynamoDB Reads Work

In a race to understand how DynamoDB reads work, our first step should be to get familiar with the central stage where all the operations take place - the DynamoDB table.

11.1. The Table: The Heart of Operations

A DynamoDB table, the nucleus of all activity, is a collection of data stored in key-value fashion. What's intriguing is that one can specify two distinct types of keys while designing their table; Partition Key and Sort Key (optional). The partition key uniquely identifies each item in the table and gets hashed by an internal hash function within DynamoDB. The outcome? A uniform distribution of data across different storage nodes, ensuring high-level efficiency in large-scale operations.

Did you ask, "What if we need a secondary access pattern within a partition?" Well, that's when the optional Sort Key jumps in, offering a sorted data structure within each partition. You add another layer of complexity, yes, but what you get in return is an enriched ability to query data.

11.2. Travelling Through the I/O Highway

Having laid the understanding foundation, now let's dive into 'reads'. At its heart, DynamoDB offers two types of reads - strongly consistent reads and eventually consistent reads.

Strongly consistent reads ensure that a read returns the result of all writes that received a successful response prior to the read. In contrast, eventually consistent reads might sometimes not reflect the results of recently completed writes instantly but promise eventual consistency as the name suggests.

You might wonder, "Does it matter?" Indeed, it does. The nature of your application will dictate the choice; if immediate consistency is a prime requirement, strongly consistent reads become your go-to. However, be aware that they might consume more capacity than their eventual counterparts. Hence, if your application tolerates eventual consistency and seeks resource efficiency, eventually consistent reads are your answer.

11.3. Units: The Fuel of DynamoDB Operations

In the milieu of reads, it's paramount to define "Read Units" or "RCU" (Read capacity units), the fuel that powers DynamoDB reads. Each RCU offers one strongly consistent read per second for items up to 4KB in size. If we are dealing with eventually consistent reads, a single RCU offers two reads per second. Thus, the size of items and the chosen type of read determine the number of RCUs consumed during a read operation.

Are there complexities? You bet. Larger items and strongly consistent reads can consume higher RCUs, potentially leading to throttling. Hence, knowing your requirements and designing your read operations accordingly becomes the secret sauce for effective DynamoDB management.

11.4. Peeling the Layers: How Throttling Works

DynamoDB works to balance resource consumption and efficient delivery, often leveraging throttling. When an operation exceeds the provisioned throughput for a table (defined by the sum of RCUs and WCUs - write capacity units) or a part of it (like a partition), DynamoDB can throttle the operation to maintain balance. A typical reaction is an 'HTTP 400 code' from DynamoDB with a 'ProvisionedThroughputExceededException' message.

Yet, DynamoDB isn't the villain of the piece here but a judicious resource manager helping you maintain resiliency. By encouraging efficient design, it motivates you to avoid scenarios that might cause increased consumption of capacity units leading to throttling.

11.5. The Saga of Hot Partitions

Another relevant term in the DynamoDB read landscape is 'hot partition'. If requests concentrate on a specific partition key, the partition can become 'hot', leading to throttled requests. Since the throughput is fixed per partition, it's of essence to avoid designing access patterns that might cause this 'hot' scenario. Distributing your workload uniformly across partition keys minimizes hot partitions and spreads resource consumption evenly.

11.6. Bursts: A Sudden Wave of Reads

Sometimes, sudden, unexpected waves of reads can occur. How does DynamoDB tolerate that? Meet Burst Capacity. Systems naturally fluctuate. Very rarely are reads consistently required at the same level. DynamoDB accumulates a few minutes of unused read and write capacity for times of sudden demand. Yet, one must remember, Burst Capacity isn't infinite. If this surplus gets exhausted, throttling might be the imminent reality.

11.7. Peeking Into the Past: DynamoDB Streams

DynamoDB Streams allows users to retrieve a time-ordered sequence of item level modifications in your DynamoDB table for the last 24 hours. So, if the need arises to track changes, DynamoDB Streams has you covered. However, remember, such enabling might increase the RCUs consumed.

11.8. Summing It Up: the Parting Notes

Grasping the mechanics of DynamoDB reads requires dancing through the realms of understanding tables, choosing the right read type, learning about RCUs, and comprehending throttling and hot partitions. Additionally, the features of Burst Capacity and DynamoDB Streams add another shade of complexity. Yet, once you pull off this dance smoothly, you realize - DynamoDB reads aren't that complex, after all. Plus, it might just be the database solution that your application sorely needs. Dive in, find out.

In the next journey, we delve into the fascinating world of DynamoDB writes. Hold on tight. More adventures await.

Chapter 12. Understanding Consistency Models: Strong Vs Eventual

A deep dive into the types of consistency models can't start without a proper introduction into what consistency actually means in database systems. As a fundamental concept, consistency in database systems is all about ensuring that any read request to the database returns the latest write operation. Here, the intricacy lies in the operative word 'latest'. What exactly does 'latest' mean in different database systems, especially when we are dealing with distributed databases? Let's explore.

12.1. What Is Consistency?

Consistency is the expectation that a read operation will reveal the most recent write operation. This implies that for any two reads of the same item, if the latter read was initiated after the former read returns, the results of that latter read will include the previous write operation. But remember, 'time' in a distributed system can have different interpretations. This is where consistency models come in to provide order and coherence.

12.2. Strong Consistency

Under strong consistency, or what we often call 'strict' or 'linearizable' consistency, the system appears as if there is only a single copy of the data. Whenever any update occurs, any subsequent attempts to read the data will reveal the update. All users see the same sequence of changes to any given item in the database, and there is a total order of all operations. This provides an ease of understanding for developers but at the cost of increased latency and lowered availability.

With strong consistency, writes are not considered successful until they propagate across all replicas. While this approach guarantees read-after-write consistency, it can significantly affect system performance, especially when dealing with geographically distributed systems where data replication can take considerable time.

12.3. Eventual Consistency

Under what we commonly call 'eventual' consistency, if no new updates are made to a particular item, eventually all reads to that item will return the same result. However, eventual consistency allows for the possibility that stale data may be read, as not all replicas are updated immediately during a write operation. Despite this, it offers a level of consistency that can be acceptable for many applications, and importantly, it allows for higher levels of system availability.

However, it's worth mentioning that eventual consistency carries the risk of inconsistency during the "eventually" period. In times of network partition or delays, some replicas may return out-of-date read results. But for many applications, this risk is outweighed by the benefits higher availability affords.

12.4. Strong Vs Eventual: Trade-offs

The debate between strong and eventual consistency boils down to system requirements and the specific trade-offs you're willing to make. For systems with high availability and partition tolerance requirements, eventual consistency often wins out despite the risk of temporary inconsistency.

On the other hand, for systems where data accuracy is of paramount importance – think financial transactions or inventory management systems – strong consistency is the preferred choice, even at the cost of slightly higher latencies.

12.5. Understanding Consistency Controls in DynamoDB

With the choice between strong and eventual consistency, DynamoDB provides flexibility. By default, it applies eventual consistency, but you do have the option to demand strong consistency. Traditionally, reads in DynamoDB (GetItem, Query, Scan operations) are eventually consistent, but if you need strongly consistent reads, you can request them.

A strongly consistent read returns a result that reflects all writes that received a successful response prior to the read. In contrast, an eventually consistent read might not reflect the results of a recently successful write. However, they generally offer better read performance.

Notably, use of strongly consistent reads may lead to higher latency or even being throttled during peak times, which is something to consider during system architecture. But rest assured, there are ways to handle these, which we will discuss in subsequent chapters.

12.6. Real-life Use Cases

To better understand the concepts of strong and eventual consistency, let's look at a few real-world use cases.

An excellent example of eventual consistency is a social media app like Twitter. Suppose you tweet and immediately after, a friend tries to view your tweet from across the world. For few seconds, your tweet might not appear due to eventual consistency, but in a social media scenario, this is acceptable.

A strongly consistent system can be seen in banking applications. If you deposit money into your bank account, a subsequent operation to check your balance must reflect that deposit. To prevent any mismatch in balance, banking systems require strong consistency.

This chapter is an introductory delve into the intriguing world of consistency models in DynamoDB. By now, the terminology should be familiar – strong consistency with its fantastic latency and smooth sequence of changes but with potentially lowered availability. Eventual consistency, offering improvements in availability and performance but with the risk of inconsistency during certain periods.

In the following chapters, we will detail more about how to handle DynamoDB consistent read issues and propose well-researched solutions to mitigate them in real-life scenarios. Stay tuned!

Chapter 13. Trouble in Paradise: Typical Errors in DynamoDB Read Operations

DynamoDB, Amazon's high-performance, fully managed NoSQL database, is typically lauded for its scalability and low-latency performance. However, no territory is without its unique troubles, and the same holds for DynamoDB - particularly concerning read operations.

Despite the product's selling point as maintaining consistent low-latency, users often bump into seemingly insurmountable consistent read issues which can feel like a thorn in their side. Understanding these common errors is half the battle towards effective remediation. Therefore, the focus of this unflinchingly honest segment rests on uncovering, understanding and resolving typical errors in DynamoDB read operations.

13.1. Understanding Consistent and Eventually Consistent Reads

Before delving into the errors, let's first understand the fundamental concepts of Consistent and Eventually Consistent Reads. In a DynamoDB GetItem operation (the primary operation to return a single item's attributes), two read options exist: Consistent Read and Eventually Consistent Read.

A Consistent Read delivers the most recent data, always reflecting a write operation that proceeded it, notwithstanding the chosen replication method between multiple Azure regions. Meanwhile, in an Eventually Consistent Read, the data return can potentially be stateless, especially if a write operation preceded it immediately.

The key differentiator between the two types lies in data duplication. A write operation often replicates to all regions within a minute. Therefore, an Eventually Consistent Read executed immediately following a write operation could pull stale or inconsistent data. Conversely, a Consistent Read circumvents this problem by only retrieving data after replication is complete.

13.2. Insufficient Throughput Provisioning

Arguably, one of the most common errors in DynamoDB read operations links back to a shortfall of read capacity units (RCU) or write capacity units (WCU), also known as ProvisionedThroughputExceededException.

DynamoDB read operations require Read Capacity Units (RCUs) as a computation unit. Each RCU represents one strongly consistent read per second or two eventually consistent reads per second, for an item up to 4 KB. If your read operations are larger, or your workloads more demanding, you may find yourself exceeding the provisioned RCUs, thereby eliciting the infamous ProvisionedThroughputExceededException error.

To resolve this, you could opt for an On-Demand throughput mode, or increase RCUs and WCUs in Provisioned throughput mode. Remember, though, that an upper limit to RCUs and WCUs exists, which if exceeded, will need a request limit increase.

13.3. Consistent Read Unavailability

Another commonly encountered error is the unavailability of consistent read operations resulting from replication delays. This usually occurs when you perform a read operation immediately after a write operation, expecting it to return the most recent data.

One solution is incorporating a delay after the write operation, giving DynamoDB sufficient time to replicate the data across all regions before performing a read. Alternatively, you can leverage DynamoDB Streams which can help synchronize the read-after-write operations by ensuring that read operations only occur after data has successfully been written and replicated.

13.4. Stale Data Reads

An Eventually Consistent Read operation occasionally fetches stale data, typically if requested immediately after a write. This isn't an error but a trade-off between performance and consistency.

To ensure fresh data, consider switching to a Consistent Read mechanism that may delay the read operation but guarantees retrieving the most recent data. Alternatively, a mechanism to implement an artificial delay post-write before invoking an eventually consistent read can ensure sufficient time for data consistency.

Despite these challenges, DynamoDB remains a powerful and highly scalable NoSQL service. Its potent potential can be unlocked by understanding the common errors and their workarounds. With this knowledge at the forefront, you can better maneuver the DynamoDB landscape, ensuring seamless and efficient database operations.

Chapter 14. The Art of Debugging Read Consistency Issues

Understanding the world of DynamoDB and the nuts and bolts of read consistency issues is crucial for anyone trying to traverse the terrain of distributed databases. This journey takes us through essential landscapes - the definitions, the causes, the symptoms, and, of course, the solutions of read consistency issues. Prepare to delve deep into some of the intricate aspects of DynamoDB and get out with a solid understanding and valuable strategies to tread DynamoDB territory.

Let's embark on this exploration, shedding light on every corner of read consistency.

14.1. Setting the Stage: Definition and Importance of Read Consistency

DynamoDB supports two types of read operations – eventually consistent and strongly consistent. An eventually consistent read means that the response might not reflect the results of a recently completed write operation due to some latency. However, a strongly consistent read can reflect all writes that received a successful response, providing the most current data. The eventual consistency models allow for higher availability and read performance, proving critical in scenarios where the application can manage with slightly stale data. Strong consistency, albeit being slightly more resource-intensive, is crucial in applications where real-time data accuracy is paramount.

Why does it matter? Data inconsistency may lead to erroneous downstream operations. Planning and management to ensure data consistency is a secret recipe for robust database architecture.

14.2. The Causes: Factors Leading to Read Consistency Issues

Understanding what factors contribute to read consistency issues can help prevent and debug issues effectively. Following are common reasons:

1. Load on the table: Too many operations can overload a table, leading to slower responses, inconsistencies, or even data loss.

2. Insufficient read capacity units (RCUs): Inadequate RCUs can choke read operations, leading to inconsistencies.

3. Network partitioning: In a distributed system, if a network partition occurs, it may lead to data inconsistency.

4. Other issues: Technical glitches, software bugs, or network issues can also contribute, causing discrepancies in the read consistency.

14.3. Symptoms: Detecting Read Consistency Issues

Detecting read inconsistencies can be challenging, given the latent nature of the symptoms. However, some indicators point towards the likelihood of issues.

1. Inconsistent Results: This could be the most apparent symptom. For instance, receiving different results for the same query in a short time frame.

2. High Latencies: Query operations taking longer than normal to

execute, especially when the load on the database is not too high, might indicate an issue.

3. Unusual Throttling: If DynamoDB is excessively throttling read requests, it might hint at a problem with the provisioned RCUs or read consistency at large.

14.4. Under the Hood: Debugging Read Consistency Issues

Debugging read consistency issues in DynamoDB involves a methodical approach. Identifying the problem, determining its source, isolating the conditions leading to the problem, and replicating the issue are the first steps towards effective debugging.

The following strategies come handy while debugging:

1. Monitor and Log: Regularly monitoring CloudWatch Metrics for DynamoDB can provide useful insights into request patterns, throttling rates, and error codes. Logs should be the first stop when diagnosing issues, presenting a real-time scenario of what's happening.

2. Review Settings: Ensure the read settings are set correctly for your use case. For example, if your application is reading data immediately after writing, strongly consistent reads are a better choice.

3. Capacity Planning: Planning the capacity units according to the requirement and load patterns can prevent consistency issues. DynamoDB Auto Scaling can be used to handle peak loads efficiently.

4. Query Execution Analysis: Comparing the execution time and results of queries under different circumstances and loads can provide valuable insights.

14.5. Solutions: Crafting an Effective Strategy

An effective strategy to address read consistency involves both corrective measures and preventive steps.

1. Optimal Use of RCUs: Increase the read capacity units (RCUs) if the current allocation is insufficient. Auto Scaling can help manage variable loads.

2. Consistent Read Selection: Choose a consistent read type wisely according to the application requirement. For eventual consistency, do read retries to mitigate the impact of inconsistencies.

3. Partition Management: Proper handling of network partitions can ensure data consistency and prevent sudden loads on a single node.

4. Using DAX (DynamoDB Accelerator): It is a caching service that delivers up to a 10x read performance improvement. It's best for read-heavy, bursty traffic patterns.

This journey, beginning from understanding the basic principles of read consistency, has enabled us to grasp every important facet, every familiar and unfamiliar alley of read consistency in DynamoDB. Debugging read consistency issues need not be a perplexing exercise anymore, with this guide illuminating this complex topic in the simplest way.

DynamoDB, once deemed challenging and complicated, is now more accessible and manageable. Remember, the understanding of one's tools is the artisan's true power. And in your hands now lies a potent instrument to master DynamoDB read consistency.

Chapter 15. Best Practice: The Right Way to Implement Consistent Reads

Dive right into the consistently challenging world of DynamoDB consistent reads may feel like traversing a stormy sea. But, with a proper grasp of the concepts and practice of the right methodologies, the voyage can turn into a rewarding excursion. A consistent read in DynamoDB refers to the read process where the most recent data write is returned, accounting for all preceding write, update or delete actions. By default, DynamoDB employs "eventually consistent" reads but also provides an option for "strongly consistent" reads according to requirements.

15.1. Strongly vs Eventually Consistent Reads

In a nutshell, a strongly consistent read returns a result reflecting all the writes up to the point when the read request was received. There's no delay. However, an eventually consistent read could return a result that doesn't account for all writes received just prior to the read action. The upside is, it consumes half the read capacity units, therefore being more cost-efficient.

Given the nature of distributed databases, there are periods when read data may appear slightly outdated due to inherent latency in data propagation. This aspect is the major distinction between the two types of reads - the level of read consistency. A clear understanding of the differences and their implications on our database operations helps us make informed decisions and use them effectively.

15.2. When to Use Which

The choice between strong and eventual consistency largely depends on the nature of your application and dataset. If your use case requires absolute real-time data, without any risk of seeing stale or outdated data, opt for strongly consistent reads. Real-time gaming, financial transactions or any other latency-sensitive operations are examples of such scenarios.

However, if your application can tolerate a small delay in data consistency in favor of reducing costs, eventually consistent reads are the better option. For instance, when showing product recommendations or user comments where a few seconds of lag won't significantly impact the user experience.

15.3. Achieving Strong Consistency

To implement strongly consistent reads in DynamoDB, you must expressly specify this during your read request since DynamoDB defaults to eventually consistent reads. Using the AWS SDK, here's how you ensure a strongly consistent read:

```
GetItemRequest request = new GetItemRequest()
    .withTableName("YourTableName")
    .withKey(new Key().withHashKeyElement(new
AttributeValue().withS("YourKeyValue")))
    .withConsistentRead(true);
```

In the above code snippet, the statement .withConsistentRead(true) guarantees a strongly consistent read.

15.4. Handling Consistency Issues

Despite its effectiveness, implementing strong consistency comes with its hurdles. Continuous strongly consistent reads can cause table throttling, increased latency, and even impact availability during network partitions.

To address this, you can make use of adaptive capacity. It allows your table to withstand uneven data access patterns or sudden bursts of read/write activity. DynamoDB automatically manages adaptive capacity, boosting your table's performance.

Another efficient strategy to tackle potential consistency problems is implementing smart partition keys. The correct partition key design can help evenly distribute data and read/write loads across many partitions, optimizing performance.

15.5. Reading from Global Secondary Indexes

Global Secondary Indexes (GSIs) provide a dynamic querying ability, but there's a twist. If you're running strongly consistent reads on a GSI, you should be aware that it won't ensure strong consistency. GSIs only support eventually consistent reads. Even so, GSIs can be a powerful tool when balanced proper with the base table reads.

To cache and return recent write data quickly, consider using DAX (DynamoDB Accelerator). It provides in-memory caching for your DynamoDB tables, making it well-suited for read-heavy workloads and reducing response times from milliseconds to microseconds, even for large datasets.

15.6. The Cost Aspect

Remember, costs are directly influenced by your choice of read consistency. A strongly consistent read costs double the amount of read capacity units (RCUs) than an eventually consistent read. So, design your database operations that suit your budget constraints without overlooking the need for data consistency.

Even though DynamoDB offers a lot under the hood to optimize costs, such as auto scaling and on-demand capacity, the right balance of read consistency is a significant contributor to managing expenditure.

15.7. Conclusion

To summarize, the right implementation of consistent reads in a DynamoDB environment hinges on a clear understanding of your data, application requirements, and read consistency principles. Making the correct choice between strong and eventual consistency, coupled with intelligent use of AWS features such as GSIs, DAX, and adaptive capacities, can transform the way you interact with your database.

Remember, DynamoDB is more about choice. There's no one-size-fits-all approach. Various applications and circumstances require different strokes of implementation. As a DynamoDB user, your primary task is to evaluate the options and weave them together to create a perfect tapestry for your specific use case.

The journey may be daunting, but with the right practices in place, consistent read issues in DynamoDB will be a roadblock of the past. Step ahead! Let the exploration continue...

Chapter 16. Roadmap to Resolution: Mitigating Read Consistency Concerns

Understanding the nature of read consistency in DynamoDB is crucial to maximizing your database's potential and countering common read consistency issues. In this broad and extensive discussion, we'll identify frequent problems and discuss several strategies for resolving them.

16.1. Understanding Read Consistency

First and foremost, you need a deep understanding of what read consistency in DynamoDB entails. In essence, it is a mode of read operation that ensures that all write operations (including updates) are reflected instantly during a read operation. Consistency across all copies of data is achieved in the span of a single read or write operation.

The system supports two types of read consistency:

1. **Strongly consistent reads**: When enabled, this feature returns a result reflecting all writes received and indexed as of the time of the read.

2. **Eventually consistent reads**: Unlike its counterpart, this mode may not reflect the result of the most recently completed write operations in your read. However, after a fraction of seconds, repeated reads should return updated data.

For mission-critical applications where real-time updates are essential, selecting a strong consistency read may be ideal. However, knowing the peculiarities of these two read consistency operations is critical because of DynamoDB's nature. By not prescribing strong consistency, DynamoDB's design aims to provide high availability and partition tolerance, but at a cost.

16.2. Common Read Consistency Problems

The problems that users often encounter with DynamoDB read consistency primarily arise from misunderstanding its nature. Here, we'll explore some common read consistency issues and their implications.

1. **Eventual consistency delays**: Although the delay for eventual consistency is typically less than a second, latency can occasionally occur due to network disruptions or high traffic. This might lead to outdated data appearing in your reads.

2. **Inconsistent data with Strong consistency**: Even with strong consistency, inconsistencies may occur due to latency or incomplete propagation. This is especially true when reading right after a write operation.

3. **Increased read cost with Strong consistency**: Strong consistency in DynamoDB uses double the read capacity units of eventual consistency. This means your allocated read capacity could drain twice as fast, leading to throttling issues, especially if your workload exceeded your provisioned capacity.

16.3. Effective Strategies to Mitigate Consistency Issues

Having identified some critical read consistency problems, it's time to discuss various strategies to mitigate these issues effectively.

1. **Anticipate and Monitor Latency**: Incorporate allowances for slight latency into your application's design if you opt for eventual consistency. Tools like Amazon CloudWatch can help you monitor latency issues.

2. **Proper Capacity Planning**: Since consuming read capacity is more in strong consistency, effective capacity planning becomes crucial. Calculating your read capacity requirements ensures your applications function without hiccups.

3. **Distributed Load**: To avoid throttling from reading heavily updated partitions, consider distributing your read load across all partitions evenly.

4. **Opt for On-Demand Capacity**: If your application faces unpredictable workloads, consider DynamoDB's On-Demand read capacity mode. It gives you the ability to serve thousands of requests per second without capacity planning.

16.4. Case Study: Managing Consistency on High Traffic Applications

Let's look at a real-life example of an application handling a surge in traffic, thus necessitating strongly consistent reads. The application initially worked with eventual consistency but migrated due to increased demand for instant updates.

To cope with this, they implemented proper capacity planning to assess their needs accurately. Also, they added more read capacity units in proportion to the traffic increase, thereby maintaining consistent performance and avoiding under-provisioning.

By setting up rules on CloudWatch, they could monitor and alert any abnormal latency, enabling them to solve hiccups before impacting the user experience profoundly. They also ensured a distributed load across all partitions, reducing throttling.

This strategic shift clearly highlights the importance of targeting DynamoDB's configuration to your application needs. It also demonstrates that, with careful management and monitoring, read consistency issues can be mitigated and even eliminated.

16.5. Wrapping Up

Read consistency is an essential aspect of DynamoDB, and understanding its nuances can greatly enhance your ability to work effectively with this powerful AWS service. Thoroughly grasping its concepts, piloting careful resolutions, and learning from real-life applications, you are now armed with requisite tools to navigate the intricacies of DynamoDB read consistency. Navigate wisely, and let your database operations thrive.

Chapter 17. Looking Ahead: Future of Read Consistency in DynamoDB

DynamoDB's advent marked a watershed moment in the database management world. Empowering developers with high-speed read and write capabilities and easy scalability, it quickly garnered attention. However, a powerful tool such as DynamoDB requires a profound understanding of its functional layers - especially read consistency - to exploit its maximum potential. As we peer into the future, we discover an intriguing landscape ripe for research and exploration, particularly regarding read consistency.

17.1. Isolating Issues: Intricacies and the Importance of Read Consistency

Fundamentally, read consistency refers to whether the most recent data update is retrievable or whether potentially outdated, inconsistent data is presented instead. This may seem insignificant on the surface, but in rapidly updating databases catering to multiple users, it can produce stark differences.

Understanding read consistency involves diving into the world of consistency models such as the `Strong Consistency Model` and `Eventually Consistent Model`. The former guarantees the return of the latest data, updated across all systems. Simultaneously, the Latter furnishes the most recently accessed data, which may not reflect the latest updates noticeably. DynamoDB provides options for both, ensuring flexibility according to specific user requirements.

It's also necessary to understand that consistent reads in DynamoDB use more capacity units than eventual ones. When planning the future of read consistency, considering this performance and cost trade-off becomes crucial.

17.2. DynamoDB's Approach: Strong Consistency and Eventual Consistency

In DynamoDB, users can choose between eventual and strongly consistent reads, depending on their application's requirements. With eventual consistency, data is immediately written to one location with the replication occurring at a slightly later time, thus it offers maximum throughput at lower costs. However, the newly written data may not be immediately accessible.

Strongly consistent reads, on the other hand, reflect all writes that received a successful response prior to the read. This guarantees that every read returns the latest data, offering a higher degree of accuracy at an increased cost. Understanding this capability and incorporating it into configurations is the key to leveraging the power of DynamoDB.

17.3. Future Perspectives

Given the significance of read consistency, let's turn our gaze toward its future in DynamoDB.

17.3.1. Advancements in Strong Consistency

We anticipate significant enhancements in strong data consistency. With the rise of real-time applications requiring immediate data accuracy, it's imperative for AWS to focus on strong consistency.

Although it currently provides this function, future upgrades, like reducing the cost and improving performance, would drive more users towards this option without fearing trade-offs.

Cross-region Strong Consistency

Currently, DynamoDB limits strong consistency to single-region access. However, future advancements foresee expanding this to global tables across multiple regions. Such improvements would mean providing precise, updated data across different geographies, a vital factor for multinational corporations and applications with a worldwide presence.

17.3.2. Innovations in Eventual Consistency

Despite the predicted surge in strong consistency demand, eventual consistency won't lose relevance. Asynchronous systems or systems that can work with slightly outdated data would continue opting for the cheaper, higher throughput option of eventual consistency.

Enhanced Replication Speed

To reduce the potential latency for data access in eventual consistency, the focus would be on accelerating the replication process. Quicker replication would mean that even eventual consistency could offer data that's nearly as accurate as strongly consistent reads, bolstering its ideal use-case scenarios.

17.4. Embracing Change: Preparing for the Future

As we brace for the forthcoming enhancements and adjustments in DynamoDB's read consistency, it's naturally prudent to prepare our systems.

Adopt a strong understanding of your application requirements, particularly in terms of data accuracy. Recognize the nuances determining the choice between eventual and strong consistency. Fluctuating factors such as cost, latency, and load may also impact your choice. Therefore, planning for scalability and building in flexibility will be paramount.

As rate of data creation accelerates, stronger consistency and faster eventual consistency become more significant. Prepare for the possibility of strong consistency becoming the default choice, especially for applications demanding immediate data accuracy.

Meanwhile, ensure your systems can handle the trade-offs involved, like potential performance reductions or increased costs. The future may necessitate a shift toward more performant hardware or optimized systems to handle increased consistency requirements.

17.5. Conclusion

The in-depth study of read consistency, captured within the folds of this broad discussion, highlights the intricacy of managing DynamoDB environments. As we gear towards a future rife with data-intensive and real-time applications, understanding these nuances will prove indispensable.

DynamoDB's evolution towards providing better mechanisms for complete data accuracy and thereby better application support is inevitable. The road ahead for read consistency in DynamoDB is expected to be a thrilling ride, replete with transformation and improvement, ensuring data accuracy like never before, and that forms the crux of understanding the future of read consistency in DynamoDB.

Made in the USA
Las Vegas, NV
27 December 2023

83570621R00026